For Clodagh Corcoran

First published 1989
by Walker Books Ltd
87 Vauxhall Walk
London SE11 5HJ

Text © 1989 Individual authors
Illustrations © 1989 Individual artists
Mother Goose logo design by Jan Pieńkowski

First printed 1989
Printed by MacLehose & Partners Ltd, Portsmouth

British Library Cataloguing in Publication Data
Ten golden years.
1. Poetry in English, 1945– – Anthologies–
For children
821'.914'0809282

ISBN 0-7445-1214-X

T·E·N GOLDEN YEARS

WALKER BOOKS
LONDON

T·E·N GOLDEN YEARS

In this anthology, Mother Goose gathers under her wings all the winners of her award, which celebrates its tenth anniversary this year. The book is a collection of new poems by many of our best contemporary poets, illustrated by some of the most talented artists for children's books to have emerged in the last decade.

The Mother Goose Award was first presented in 1979 and is given to "the most outstanding newcomer" to children's book illustration in Britain. It was set up by the bookseller and critic, Clodagh Corcoran, when she brought together a panel of judges who shared both her enthusiasm for illustration and her conviction of its importance in children's books. What makes the award special is that it comes at the outset of an illustrator's professional life – encouragement for a career that's just beginning, rather than fully established.

Our thanks are due to the poets; to the artists who freely contributed their work to this anthology; to our sponsors, Books for Children book club, for underwriting the whole enterprise and for supporting the award so generously since 1983; and to our publisher, Walker Books, who gave invaluable editorial and design advice at every stage.

The royalties from *Ten Golden Years* will go towards parents' accommodation at the Hospital for Sick Children, Great Ormond Street, London – a tribute, as it were, from Mother Goose to Peter Pan.

for the Mother Goose Award

MOTHER GOOSE
AWARD WINNERS

1979
MICHELLE CARTLIDGE

1980
REG CARTWRIGHT

1981
JUAN WIJNGAARD

1982
JAN ORMEROD

1983
SATOSHI KITAMURA

1984
PATRICK BENSON

1985
SUSAN VARLEY

1986
NOT AWARDED

1987
PATRICK LYNCH

1988
EMMA CHICHESTER CLARK

1989
CHARLES FUGE

RATTiN 'iT UP

C'mon everybody
Slap some grease on those paws
Get some yellow on your teeth
And, uh, sharpen up your claws

There's a whole lot of sausage
We're gonna swallow down
We're gonna jump out the sewers
And rock this town

Cos we're rattin' it up
Yes we're rattin' it up
Well we're rattin' it up
For a ratting good time tonight!

Ain't got no compass
You don't need no map
Just follow your snout
Hey, watch out for that trap!

You can take out a poodle
Beat up a cat
But if you can't lick a ferret
You ain't no kind of rat

Cos we're rattin' it up
Yes we're rattin' it up
Well we're rattin' it up
For a ratting good time tonight!

Now you can sneak in the henhouse
You can roll out the eggs
But if the farmer comes running
Bite his hairy legs

Check that cheese for poison
Before you eat
Or you'll wind up being served up
As ratburger meat

Cos we're rattin' it up
Yes we're rattin' it up
Well we're rattin' it up
For a ratting good time tonight!

This rat was born to rock
This rat was born to roll
I don't give a monkey's
'Bout your pest control

So push off pussy-cat
And push off pup
We're the Rocking Rodents
And we're ratting it up

Yeah we're rattin' it up
Yeah we're rattin' it up
Well we're rattin' it up
For a ratting good time tonight!

Adrian Mitchell

Patrick Blason

"NICE TO SEE THE BOYS PLAYING SO WELL TOGETHER"

I'll sting you with my tonsilizor,
Sting! Sting!
    I'll blast you into chickenpox,
    Blast! Blast!
I'll zap you into molly cules,
Zap! Zap!
    I'll flatten you with my inter-galactic cruncher,
    Flatten! Flatten!
I'll scrunch you with my monster-bomb,
Scrunch! Scrunch!
    I'll exterminate you with my exterminator-ray,
    Exterminate! Exterminate!
I'll blap you with my meat-seeking missile,
Blap! Blap!
    I'll sock you with my horror-blaster,
    Sock! Sock!
I'll horror you with my sock-blaster,
Horror! Horror!
    I'll wipe you off the face of the planet!
Then I'll wipe you off the face of the galaxy!
    And I'll wipe you off the face of the universe!
Well, I'll, I'll punch you in the nose!

"Mummy! Mummy! Billy says he's gonna punch me in the nose!"

Colin McNaughton

The Lobster

Hear the Lobster's song:
"Not everybody's been a
Dainty Ballerina
Armoured like a Knight.
At a dance, at a fight
I was a thrilling sight.
But O not for long.

It was the stupid sea,
The fumbling, mumbling sea,
The sea took me apart
And lost my clever wits
And lost my happy heart
And then jammed all my bits
Back together wrong.
Now I'm just a fright.
I don't know what to do.
I'm feeling pretty blue."

Ted Hughes

Caterpillar

Once a chubby caterpillar
Sat upon a leaf,
Singing, "Eat, eat and be merry –
Life is very brief."

Soon he lost his appetite
And changed his merry tune.
He started spinning, hid himself
Inside a hard cocoon.

And he was still and quiet there –
Day after day went by.
At last it cracked and he emerged,
A gorgeous butterfly.

He spread his brown and crimson wings
And warmed them in the sun
And sang, "Now I must see the world –
My life has just begun."

Wendy Cope

April Poem

The morning moon is round and gold

Up in the misty milk-blue sky;

The towering poplar sways alone;

The birds are shouting one by one,

It's first of April, everyone!

In April foolery, that moon

Shines like a small and gentle sun.

Gerda Mayer

Susan Varley 13

THE DARK

I don't like the dark coming down on my head

It feels like a blanket thrown over the bed

I don't like the dark coming down on my head

I don't like the dark coming down over me

It feels like the room's full of things I can't see

I don't like the dark coming down over me

There isn't enough light from under the door

It only just reaches the edge of the floor

There isn't enough light from under the door

I wish that my dad hadn't put out the light

It feels like there's something that's just out of sight

I wish that my dad hadn't put out the light

But under the bedclothes it's warm and secure

You can't see the ceiling you can't see the floor

Yes, under the bedclothes it's warm and secure

So I think I'll stay here till it's daylight once more.

Adrian Henri

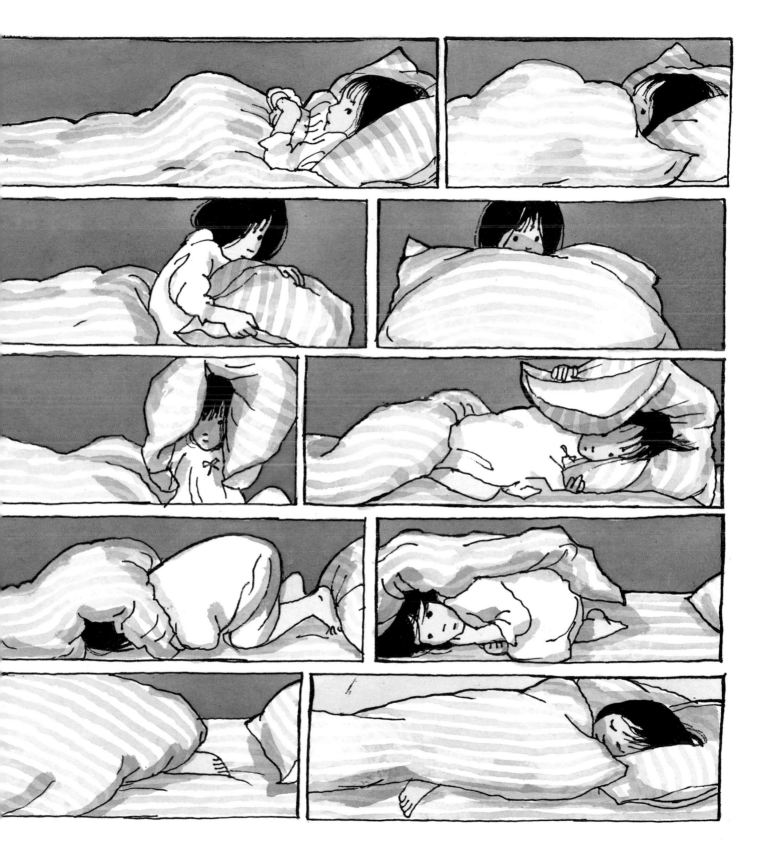

HAPPY DOGDAY

Today –
Is our dog's birthday.

It's Happydogdayday.
Sixteen years of panting
And sixteen years of play.

Sixteen years of dogtime.
Sixteen years of barks
– eating smelly dog food
And making muddy marks.

It's a hundred years of our time.
It's a hundred human years
– of digging in the garden
And scratching itchy ears.

A hundred years of living rooms
(he never goes upstairs)
And dropping hairy whiskers
And being pushed off chairs.

It's a hundred years of being with us
A hundred years of Dad
And a hundred years of my sister
(that must be really bad!)

So:

No wonder he looks really old

No wonder he is grey

And cannot hear

Or jump

Or catch

Or even run away.

No wonder that he sleeps all day

No wonder that he's fat

And only dreams of catching things

And chasing neighbours' cats.

So fight your fights
In dogdream nights
Deep within your bed ...

today's your day

and we all say ...

Happy Birthday!

FRED   *Peter Dixon*

Cheeky Lee Babcott

Cheeky Lee Babcott
was a bad lad
when he asked to push a trolley
round the store for his dad.
It happened on his birthday –
he'd just turned four,
but he wouldn't be a big boy:
THAT was a bore!

The woman at the counter
had just cut the cheese
when cheeky Lee Babcott
drenched it with a sneeze.
He scowled at the customers,
sticking out his tongue,
till they tutted at the manners
of one so young.

A tired store assistant
had spent a whole hour
stacking tins of beans
into a five-feet tower.
The customers would take them
tin by tin –
well, that was the idea
till Lee trolleyed in.

Crash! went the trolley.
The beans went west,
the assistant went pale
then went for a rest.
The prices on the tins
were reduced ten pence –
it wasn't worth the hassle
of knocking out the dents.

Cheeky Lee Babcott
thought it was fun
to disarm another shopgirl
of her pricing gun:
he stuck a label on his forehead
then trolleyed down the aisle
heading for the checkout
with a gloating smile.

He hurtled in his trolley
through the exit door
and from that day to this
he's been seen no more.
Cheeky Lee's gone into hiding
and people have said
that he's out there somewhere
with a price on his head.

Michael McHugh

Miranda Mary Piker

Oh, Miranda Mary Piker

How could anybody like her?

Such a rude and disobedient little kid.

So we said, "Why don't we fix her

In the Peanut-Brittle Mixer,

Then we're sure to like her better than we did."

Soon this child who was so vicious

Will have gotten quite delicious

And her father will have surely understood

That instead of saying, "Miranda!

Oh, the beast! I cannot stand her!"

He'll be saying, "Oh, how *crunchy* and how *good*!"

Roald Dahl

19

Connie and

Early one white winter's morn,
Came Connie and her unicorn.
She knocked upon the great front door
Of greedy giant Gobblemore.

  The giant, stirring from his bed,
Rubbed both his eyes and scratched his head:
"Who is it dares wake Gobblemore?"
He roared whilst answering the door.
And who should stand there all forlorn,
But Connie and her unicorn.

  Now though he'd gorged the night before,
He hungered still, did Gobblemore;
Thought he, Oh, unicorns are sweet,
And how I yearn to eat that meat!
So, "Dear child, please come in!" he cried.
And thus did Connie go inside.

  Her face was thin, her clothes were torn,
But plumpish was her unicorn.
"Dear child what have you come here for?"
Asked the sly giant Gobblemore.
(And as he spoke, he noticed that
Her unicorn was nice and fat!)

  "Oh sir, I'm sorry," Connie said,
"I come to beg a crust of bread.
I have no money, but I trust
You'll let me have a little crust."

  Said Gobblemore (who wasn't kind
And had but one thought in his mind):
"If you've no gold to pay the debt,
Just let me have that freakish pet!"

  At such a thought the girl felt sad –
Her unicorn was all she had –
But as she hung her head in woe,
She saw she had no choice, and so
Although her heart was sadly torn,
She sighed, "Farewell, my unicorn."
And with these words, she swapped her beast

her Unicorn

For one extremely frugal feast –
Her crust of bread was far from large
And spread with just the merest marge.

   Meanwhile the giant scoured a book
To find the nicest way to cook
A unicorn: fried, boiled or stewed,
Or grilled or baked or barbecued?

   When Connie saw the giant take
Her unicorn away to bake,
She realised at once his aim
And thought she'd try and stop his game:
She grabbed a saucepan from a shelf,
And closed her eyes and braced herself,
Then flung it, hardly thinking that
She'd hit him – but she knocked him flat!

   With Gobblemore now out stone cold,
Shy Connie was a bit more bold –
She dragged the giant round the floor
And kicked him out his own back door,
Then pushed him to the icy well
And made quite sure that in he fell.

   Then with her unicorn she went
And raided his establishment:
They ate up all that they could find
And didn't leave a scrap behind –
Ate every leg of beef and ham,
Ate every slice of bread and jam,
Ate every beetroot, every bean –
They even licked their platters clean.
And every goblet, every cup,
They drank them down and drank them up.

   It took all day and half the night
To eat up everything in sight,
And when at last they both were sure
There really wasn't any more,
They left, full up, at crack of dawn,
Did Connie and her unicorn.

Colin West

Emma Chichester Clark

21

THE DUSTY GRAN

Dust was lying very thick,

Upon my granny's shooting stick,

Thicker still upon the stair,

And on my granny's silver hair.

From her dust-encrusted knees,

Fell a plate of bread and cheese,

And from my granny's feeble lips,

Came a string of racing tips,

Her dusty fingers grabbed my frock,

"It's Jack the Lad in the three o'clock."

"But how are you, dear Gran," I cried.

"Ah, not so dusty," she replied.

Pam Ayres

Reg Cartwright

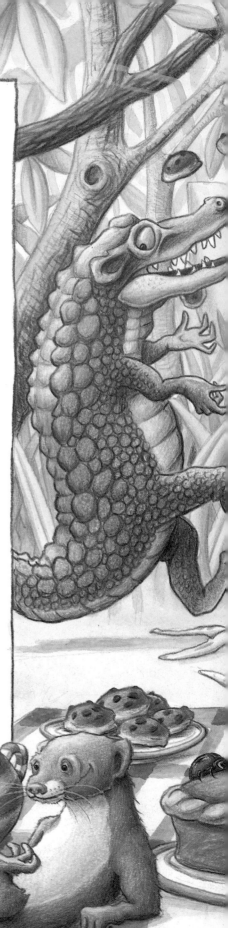

BEARS DON'T LIKE BANANAS

Monkeys like to play the drums,
        badgers wear bandanas.
Tigers like to tickle toes
        but bears don't like bananas.

        A crocodile can juggle buns
                on visits to his nana's.
        Seagulls like to dance and sing
                but bears don't like bananas.

Rats and mice can somersault
        and do gymnastics with iguanas.
Weasels like to wiggle legs
        but bears don't like bananas.

        A porcupine likes drinking tea,
                and cheering at gymkhanas.
        A ladybird likes eating pies
                but bears don't like bananas.

Charles Fuge

THE SNOWMAN

Child's play:

  stacked snow,

    scarf, hat,

      carrot nose,

        stick and

         round pebbles

          for eyes.

           He freezes:

        fat target

        for snowballers

      who dearly

     want to

    knock off

   his block.

Three days,

  and grey

    with age

      he shrinks

        as warmth

         turns the

          world green.

           Scarf, hat,

         are reclaimed.

       Pebbles mark

      his grave,

     damp lawn

    where a

   child plays.

Wes Magee

26

THE MIDNIGHT SKATERS

It is midnight in the ice-rink
And all is cool and still.
Darkness seems to hold its breath,
Nothing moves, until

Out of the kitchen, one by one,
The cutlery comes creeping,
Quiet as mice to the brink of the ice
While all the world is sleeping.

Then suddenly a serving spoon
Switches on the light,
And the silver swoops upon the ice
Screaming with delight.

The knives are high-speed skaters,
Round and round they race,
Blades hissing, sissing,
Whizzing at a dizzy pace.

Forks twirl like dancers
Pirouetting on the spot.
Teaspoons (who take no chances)
Hold hands and giggle a lot.

All night long the fun goes on
Until the sun, their friend,
Gives the warning signal
That all good things must end.

So they slink back to the kitchen
For forty winks in the drawer
And steel themselves to wait
Until it's time to skate once more.

At eight the canteen ladies
Breeze in as good as gold
To lay the tables and wonder
Why the cutlery is so cold.

Roger McGough

27

FISHY

Great Uncle Morissey, Dad and Mum
Were drowsing in deck-chairs in the sun.
"Run off and play," they said to me,
"Make sand pies till it's time for tea."

I was fetching some water in my pail
When I came across a lady with a long fishy tail,
Sitting by a pool on a seaweedy shelf,
Singing softly, all by herself.

When I asked if she'd care to take some tea
With Great Uncle Morissey, Dad, Mum and me,
She lashed up the water, shook out her hair,
Sent a thousand droplets into the air,
And I just caught sight of the tip of her fin
As she whisked up her tail and dived right in.

When I asked Uncle Morissey if he would wish
To meet a lady who was half a fish,
He only yawned and said he'd seen plenty,
When he was a lad, back in 1920.

Shirley Hughes

Patrick Benson

GRUMBLYMOON

"TURN THAT MUSIC DOWN!"

yelled the grumblymoon

to the rock

and

roll

star.

Brian Patten

SATOSHI

COWBOY MOVIES

On cowboy movies
they show you Indians as baddies
and cowboys as goodies

but think again please;

who disturb de dreams
of de sleeping wigwam
who come with de guns
going blam blam blam?

Think again please.

John Agard

DE BEAT

De beat of de drum
is a living heart

De skin of de drum
is a living goat

De wood of de drum
is a living tree

De belly of de drum
is de call of de sea

De dum of de drum is me.

Grace Nichols

BUZZ ALONG

The flight
of the
bee
seems
erratic
to me
with
a buzz
and a
flutter
of wings.
If you're
wise
let it
pass
through the
hedgerows
and grass

and
up
It is
stings.
that
section
a small
for it has

This insect,
never shrinks
from work
of day.
This insect
coming
at the

away

Through
the sun
and
the shower
it
will
visit
each
flower
that
is
serving
delectable
drinks.

Max Fatchen

Susan Varley

Haiku

Shimmering heat waves,

    A hot pebble in the hand,

        Light-dance on the sea.

Wendy Cope

How  You

Your mum or dad brings a huge box

For packing everything that's small,

And stuff that rattles: plates and crocks,

And ornaments from off the wall,

And things you wrap in cloths because

They'd break, and vases from the shelves,

And oddments from the sideboard drawers –

And this you do all by yourselves,

But one March morning, three or four

Removal men come with their van,

And set to work to load all your

Big beds and tables (one strong man

Carries the fridge out on his own)

And suddenly there's nothing there!

Each room seems just as if it's grown

To twice its size. The house *sounds* bare.

Move House

They dump the large things deep inside

The lorry first, and then they take

Your box, and heave it up beside

The rest, and still they need to make

    Space for your curtains, clothes and books,

    While back indoors you notice that

    It's not your home, the whole place looks

    Too light ... And then you seize the cat,

    And drive off to the new house, where

    They've worked so fast, you can't remember

    These rooms of furniture were bare

    When you first called here, in December.

And then you wander round and see

The things you brought, they all appear

A little strange. Those chairs must be

The same chairs; but they're *different* here ...

Alan Brownjohn

Michelle Cartlidge

37

THE CASTLE

There's a castle under the table in the lounge
With bats and owls;
Its walls may look like cardboard
And its doors like bathroom towels,
But that is just a trick to fool the dragons' beady eyes
For the castle under the table in the lounge
Is in disguise.

There's a castle under the table in the lounge
With one dark cell
Where every day my wizard, Wex,
Invents a different spell.
Today it's one to turn invaders slowly into stone;
There's a castle under the table in the lounge:
Leave it alone!

There's a castle under the table in the lounge
With steps that go
Through miles of smoky nothingness
To secret caves below
Where blacksmiths forge intruder-traps that snap with teeth of tin;
There's a castle under the table in the lounge:
You can't come in!

There's a castle under the table in the lounge
With seven towers
Where seven fair princesses sing
To seven lutes for hours,
And seven servants guard their doors with seven snarling hounds;
There's a castle under the table in the lounge;
It's out of bounds!

There's a castle under the table in the lounge
In which I hide
While dragons calling, "Tea-time! Tea-time!"
Lumber by outside –
As if I'd fall for that one, no, I'm staying here all day,
In my castle under the table in the lounge,
So keep away!

Richard Edwards

38

THE SLOTH

Now the Sloth is both unhurried
And affects a fearful frown.
This is not because he's worried
But because he's upside down.

If the passer-by inverts him
It is patent in a while
That the strange position hurts him,
For the Sloth begins to smile.

Dick King-Smith

THE AMERICAN ELK

The American Elk – also known as the wapiti –
Runs through the maple woods, clippety-cloppety.
Favoured with feet of remarkable property
Wapitis never have need of chiropody.

Dick King-Smith

Emma Chichester Clark

41

SAM GROOM

What are you writing down there, Sam Groom,
All alone in a deep, damp room,
Nose on the paper, tongue held tight,
What are you writing by candle-light?
> *Words, says Sam.*
> *That's what I am.*

Why do you write down there, Sam Groom,
While the bright bees buzz and the roses bloom?
Scribble and scrape goes your pen all day
As the sun and summer waste away.

Are you writing to your mammy or your daddy, Sam Groom,
Squinting your eye in the candle-fume,
To your brother or your sister or your own true-dove
Or a friend or a foe that we know not of?

Is it a sermon or a bill of sale,
A shilling-shocker or a nursery-tale?
Is it blank, blank verse or a tally of rhymes
Or a letter to the Editor of *The Times*?

Are you putting the wrongs to rights, Sam Groom,
As you sit in a kitchen as chill as the tomb?
Is it songs for the owl or songs for the lark
Or a tune to whistle against the dark?

They say that you'll stay where you are, Sam Groom,
From half past nothing to the day of doom.
What are you writing down there, Sam Groom,
All alone in a deep, damp room?
> *Words, says Sam.*
> *That's what I am.*

Charles Causley

Reg Cartwright

AFTER DARK

Where are you going?

ROUND THE PARK.

When are you back?

AFTER DARK.

Won't you be scared?

DON'T BE DAFT.

A ghost'll get you.

WHAT A LAUGH!

I know where it lives.

NO YOU DON'T.

And you'll run away.

NO I WON'T.

It got *me* once.

IT DIDN'T – DID IT?

It's all slimy.

'TISN'T, IS IT?

Where are you going?

I'M STAYING AT HOME.

Aren't you going to the park?

NOT ON MY OWN.

Michael Rosen

TIMELESS

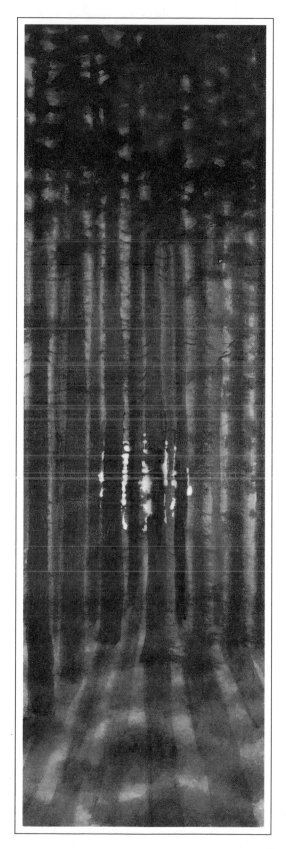

There is no clock in the forest
but a dandelion to blow,
an owl that hunts
when the light has gone,
a mouse that sleeps
till night has come,
lost in the moss below.

There is no clock in the forest,
only the cuckoo's song
and the thin white
of the early dawn,
the pale damp-bright
of a waking June,
the bluebell light
of a day half-born
when the stars have gone.

There is no clock in the forest.

Judith Nicholls